ECHOES OF ETHIOPIA: A BRIEF HISTORY

Unveiling the Majesty and Resilience of Ethiopia

ALOK SHARMA

Echoes of Ethiopia: A Brief History

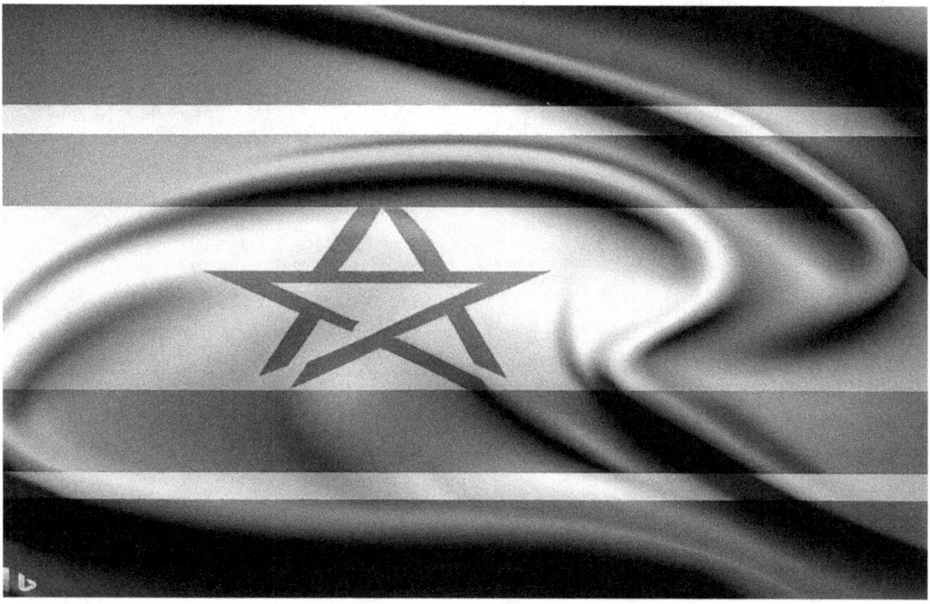

Copyright © Year 2023 by Alok Sharma

All rights reserved. No part of this publication may be reproduced, distributed, or transmitted in any form or by any means, including photocopying, recording, or other electronic or mechanical methods, without the prior written permission of the author, except in the case of brief quotations embodied in critical reviews and certain other noncommercial uses permitted by copyright law.

This book is intended for educational and informational purposes only. The author and publisher have made every effort to ensure the accuracy of the information herein. However, the author and publisher do not warrant or represent that the information provided in this book is complete, accurate, or up to date. The author and publisher disclaim any liability for any errors, omissions, or inaccuracies in the content of this book or any loss or damages arising from the use or reliance upon the information contained herein.

Any views or opinions expressed in this book are solely those of the author and do not necessarily represent the views of any third party mentioned in the book.

Cover image: Copyright

ISBN:
Printed and bound in India
First Edition: 2023

For permissions, inquiries, or feedback regarding this book, please contact the author at:

Alok Sharma
New Delhi, 11001, India
Contact Details: +91-8668957003
aloksharma07@gmail.com

"Ethiopia stretches out her hands unto God, and God stretches out His hands unto her." - Emperor Haile Selassie

"Ethiopia is a land whose praise is sung in the Scriptures." - Nelson Mandela

"Ethiopia, the land of origins, the cradle of humanity, the keeper of ancient treasures." - Unknown

"In Ethiopia, one can feel the heartbeat of Africa, the pulse of humanity." - Alemayehu Eshete

"Ethiopia is a mosaic of cultures, a tapestry of traditions, and a testament to the endurance of a proud nation." - Unknown

"Ethiopia is not just a country; it's a feeling, an experience that stays with you forever." - Unknown

"Ethiopia is a symphony of colors, a harmony of voices, and a dance of traditions." - Unknown

"Ethiopia's history is a testament to the resilience and strength of its people, who have overcome challenges and preserved their heritage with pride." - Unknown

"Ethiopia, where ancient wonders meet modern aspirations, and where the echoes of history resound through the vibrant rhythms of daily life." - Unknown

"Ethiopia is a land of legends, where stories of kings and queens, warriors and scholars, weave a tapestry of greatness." – Unknown

Ethiopia is a land of contrasts, where towering mountains and fertile valleys coexist, and where tradition and innovation blend harmoniously." - Unknown

"Ethiopia, a beacon of hope and inspiration, where the past is revered, the present is embraced, and the future is envisioned with unwavering optimism." - Unknown

"Ethiopia's cultural heritage is a treasure trove of wisdom, artistry, and beauty, captivating the hearts of those who seek to understand its depth." - Unknown

"Ethiopia, where the rhythm of the drum echoes the heartbeat of a nation, and the melodies of ancient instruments tell stories of a timeless legacy." - Unknown

"In Ethiopia, the sun rises over ancient ruins, casting a golden glow upon a land that has withstood the test of time." - Unknown

"Ethiopia, a land where hospitality is a way of life, where strangers are welcomed with open arms and treated as honored guests." - Unknown

"Ethiopia, a cradle of civilization, where the roots of humanity run deep and the spirit of exploration thrives." - Unknown

"Ethiopia's landscapes, from the rugged highlands to the vast Rift Valley, evoke a sense of awe and remind us of nature's boundless beauty." - Unknown

"Ethiopia, a mosaic of languages, customs, and traditions, where diversity is celebrated as a source of strength and unity." - Unknown

"In Ethiopia, time slows down, allowing us to savor the present moment and appreciate the simple joys of life." – Unknown

These below quotes by Alok Sharma reflect his appreciation for Ethiopia's rich history, cultural heritage, and natural beauty, inviting readers to embark on a transformative journey of exploration and understanding:

"Ethiopia is a living testament to the power of heritage, where ancient civilizations continue to shape the present and inspire the future."

"Exploring Ethiopia is like embarking on a treasure hunt, with each step revealing hidden gems of history and culture."

"In the land of Ethiopia, the past dances hand in hand with the present, creating a symphony of tradition and progress."

"Ethiopia's vibrant tapestry of cultures is a reminder of the beauty and strength that comes from embracing diversity."

"To understand Ethiopia is to unravel the threads of humanity's shared story, where the roots of civilization run deep."

"Ethiopia's landscapes are a canvas painted by nature, where breathtaking beauty unfolds at every turn."

"Ethiopia is a place where time seems to stand still, allowing us to witness the echoes of history whispering through the winds."

"Ethiopia's people embody resilience, grace, and a sense of community that is both humbling and inspiring."

"Ethiopia's historical sites are like portals to the past, inviting us to step into the footsteps of ancient civilizations and witness their greatness."

"Exploring Ethiopia is an invitation to broaden our horizons, challenge our assumptions, and discover the incredible diversity of our world."

Dedicated To

This book is dedicated to the resilient people of Ethiopia, whose unwavering spirit and rich cultural heritage have shaped the nation's history and continue to inspire generations. It is dedicated to those who have worked tirelessly to preserve Ethiopia's ancient treasures, protect its natural landscapes, and promote sustainable development for a better future.

To the historians, scholars, and researchers who have devoted their lives to unraveling the mysteries of Ethiopia's past and sharing their knowledge with the world, this book is dedicated to you. Your passion for discovery and your commitment to preserving historical accuracy have paved the way for a deeper understanding of Ethiopia's remarkable journey.

To the everyday heroes—the farmers, artisans, musicians, and storytellers—who have kept Ethiopia's traditions alive, passing them down through generations, this book is dedicated to you. Your unwavering dedication to cultural preservation has ensured that Ethiopia's vibrant heritage thrives and continues to captivate the world.

To the visionaries and leaders who have guided Ethiopia through periods of change and transformation, this book is dedicated to you. Your efforts to foster progress, alleviate poverty, improve education and healthcare, and champion gender equality have left an indelible mark on the nation's trajectory.

To the travelers and explorers who have ventured to Ethiopia's ancient lands, seeking to understand its history and connect with its people, this book is dedicated to you. Your curiosity, open-mindedness, and willingness to embrace new cultures have contributed to the cultural exchange that enriches us all.

Lastly, this book is dedicated to the future generations of Ethiopia. May they inherit a land that embraces its past, celebrates its diversity, and continues to strive for progress and unity. May they find inspiration in the stories told within these pages, and may they carry the torch of Ethiopia's legacy forward, creating a brighter and more inclusive future for all.

To all those who have played a part in shaping Ethiopia's history and those who seek to uncover its untold stories, this book is dedicated with gratitude and admiration. May it serve as a tribute to the remarkable journey of Ethiopia and as an invitation to the world to explore and appreciate its unparalleled heritage.

About the Author

Alok Sharma, the author of "Ethiopia: A Brief History," is a passionate explorer, researcher, and storyteller with a deep fascination for the diverse cultures and histories that shape our world. His insatiable curiosity led him to embark on an extraordinary journey to Ethiopia, where he immersed himself in the rich tapestry of this captivating nation.

During his time in Ethiopia, Alok Sharma spent countless hours traversing the ancient landscapes, engaging with local communities, and delving into the depths of the country's history. From the bustling streets of Addis Ababa to the remote villages nestled in the mountains, he sought to grasp the essence of Ethiopia's past and present, to understand its complexities and nuances, and to capture its spirit on the pages of this book.

Alok's firsthand experiences and interactions with Ethiopian historians, scholars, and everyday people provided him with invaluable insights into the country's traditions, challenges, and aspirations. His dedication to unearthing the hidden stories, shedding light on lesser-known aspects of Ethiopian history, and honoring the cultural diversity of the nation shines through in the pages of this book.

As a seasoned writer and researcher, Alok Sharma has dedicated his life to exploring the world's diverse cultures and histories, striving to bridge gaps in understanding and fostering a greater appreciation for the richness of human heritage. Through his meticulous research, vivid storytelling, and deep respect for the subject matter, Alok endeavors to bring the captivating history of Ethiopia to life for readers around the globe.

"Ethiopia: A Brief History" is a testament to Alok Sharma's passion for exploration, his commitment to thorough research, and his unwavering dedication to sharing the stories of the world's remarkable cultures. It is his hope that this book will ignite the curiosity and inspire a deeper appreciation for the fascinating history of Ethiopia, inviting readers to embark on their own journeys of discovery and understanding.

With Alok Sharma as your guide, prepare to be captivated by the vivid tapestry of Ethiopia's past, present, and future—a land that has captured the author's heart and left an indelible mark on his soul.

Preface: Unveiling the Ancient Tapestry of Ethiopia

Welcome to the captivating journey through the pages of "Ethiopia: A Brief History." As you embark on this literary adventure, prepare to be transported to a land steeped in ancient mystique, vibrant traditions, and a rich tapestry of history. This book serves as a gateway to unlocking the secrets of a nation that has flourished for millennia, leaving an indelible mark on the world stage.

Imagine standing on the rugged cliffs of the Ethiopian highlands, gazing upon the majestic rock-hewn churches of Lalibela, or traversing the ancient trading routes that once connected civilizations. Picture yourself immersed in the enchanting sounds of traditional music and the mesmerizing rhythms of traditional dance, resonating through the bustling streets and vibrant marketplaces. Experience the indomitable spirit of a people who have weathered the storms of history with unwavering resilience and pride.

"Ethiopia: A Brief History" invites you to delve into the origins of this extraordinary nation, tracing its roots back to ancient civilizations and exploring the dynamic interactions with foreign powers throughout the ages. From the Aksumite Empire to the medieval dynasties, from Portuguese encounters to Ethiopian isolation, from modernization to political struggles, and from cultural heritage to the challenges and progress of the 21st century, each chapter unravels a different facet of Ethiopia's compelling narrative.

As you turn the pages, you will encounter remarkable tales of emperors and conquerors, discover the profound influence of religion and spirituality, witness the ebb and flow of political power, and marvel at the diverse tapestry of cultures that have shaped this land. You will witness the clash of civilizations, the emergence of new ideas, and the continuous quest for identity and self-determination.

Beyond the historical accounts, this book celebrates the vibrant traditions, breathtaking landscapes, and the enduring spirit of the Ethiopian people. It shines a light on the efforts to preserve cultural heritage, promote sustainability, and foster progress in an ever-changing world.

Whether you are an avid history enthusiast, a curious traveler, or someone seeking to deepen their understanding of this remarkable nation, "Ethiopia: A Brief History" invites you to embark on a transformative journey. Join us as we unravel the intricate threads of Ethiopia's past, weaving together stories of triumph, struggle, and the unyielding spirit of a nation that has left an indelible mark on the tapestry of human civilization.

Prepare to be captivated, inspired, and enlightened as you uncover the fascinating narrative of Ethiopia—a land where ancient wonders meet modern aspirations, where tradition dances with innovation, and where the echoes of history resonate through the vibrant rhythms of daily life.

So, dear reader, immerse yourself in the pages that follow, as we embark on a grand odyssey through time, tracing the footsteps of the ancient Ethiopians, and rediscovering the enduring legacy of a nation that has shaped the course of history.

Welcome to the incredible tale of Ethiopia—where the past unfolds, the present beckons, and the future awaits.

Table of Contents

Echoes of Ethiopia: A Brief History 1

Dedicated To 0

Table of Contents

- About the Author 2
- Preface: Unveiling the Ancient Tapestry of Ethiopia 4
- Table of Contents 6
- Introduction 14
- Chapter 1: Origins and Ancient Civilizations 15
  - Introduction: 15
  - 1.1 The Cradle of Humanity: 15
  - 1.2 The Aksumite Empire: 15
    - 1.2.1 Rise to Power and Aksum's Golden Age: 15
    - 1.2.2 Trade Routes and the Red Sea: 16
    - 1.2.3 The Enigma of the Ark of the Covenant: 16
  - 1.3 Lalibela and the Rock-Hewn Churches: 16
  - Conclusion: 16
- Chapter 2: Medieval Dynasties and Religious Heritage 17
  - Introduction: 17
  - 2.1 The Solomonic Dynasty: 17
    - 2.1.1 Legend of the Queen of Sheba: 17
    - 2.1.2 The Kingdom of Axum: 17
  - 2.2 Orthodox Christianity: 18
    - 2.2.1 The Ethiopian Orthodox Tewahedo Church: 18
    - 2.2.2 Monasticism and Religious Centers: 18
  - 2.3 The Zagwe Dynasty and the Rock-Cut Churches in Lalibela: 18
    - 2.3.1 Lalibela's Eleven Churches: 18
  - Conclusion: 18
- Chapter 3: Portuguese Interactions and Ethiopian Isolation 20
  - 3.1 The Arrival of the Portuguese: 20
    - 3.1.1 Jesuit Missions and Religious Encounters: 20
    - 3.1.2 The Introduction of Firearms: 20
  - 3.2 The Ethiopian Empire and its Resistance against European Colonization: 21
    - 3.2.1 Emperor Menelik II and the Battle of Adwa: 21
    - 3.2.2 Emperor Haile Selassie and the League of Nations: 21

3.3 Ethiopian Isolation: 21

   3.3.1 Internal Struggles and Political Instability: 21

   3.3.2 The Era of Meles Zenawi and the Ethiopian People's Revolutionary Democratic Front (EPRDF): 21

Conclusion: 22

Chapter 4: Modernization and Political Struggles 23

Introduction: 23

4.1 Emperor Haile Selassie: 23

   4.1.1 Modernization Efforts: 23

   4.1.2 Italian Occupation and the League of Nations: 23

4.2 The Derg Regime and the Red Terror: 23

   4.2.1 Human Rights Abuses and Famine: 24

4.3 The Ethiopian People's Revolutionary Democratic Front (EPRDF) and Meles Zenawi: 24

   4.3.1 Democratization and Ethnic Federalism: 24

   4.3.2 Economic Growth and Development: 24

4.4 Challenges and Protests in the 21st Century: 24

Conclusion: 24

Chapter 5: Cultural Heritage and Diversity 26

Introduction: 26

5.1 Ethiopian Cuisine: 26

   5.1.1 Coffee Culture: 26

5.2 Ethiopian Literature: 26

5.3 Music and Dance: 27

5.4 Artistic Traditions: 27

5.5 Cultural Festivals and Celebrations: 27

Conclusion: 27

Chapter 6: Challenges and Progress in the 21st Century 28

Introduction: 28

6.1 Economic Growth and Development: 28

   6.1.1 Infrastructure Development: 28

6.2 Social and Political Challenges: 28
    6.2.1 Ethnic Tensions and Conflicts: 29
    6.2.2 Human Rights and Press Freedom: 29
6.3 Democratic Reforms: 29
    6.3.1 The Nobel Peace Prize and Regional Diplomacy: 29
6.4 Environmental Conservation and Climate Change: 29
    6.4.1 Sustainable Agriculture and Food Security: 29
Conclusion: 30

Chapter 7: Education and Human Development 31
Introduction: 31
7.1 Historical Overview of Education in Ethiopia: 31
7.2 Challenges in Education: 31
    7.2.1 Access to Education: 31
    7.2.2 Quality of Education: 32
7.3 Government Initiatives and Reforms: 32
    7.3.1 Universal Primary Education: 32
    7.3.2 Technical and Vocational Education and Training (TVET): 32
7.4 Higher Education and Research: 32
7.5 Women's Empowerment and Gender Equality: 32
Conclusion: 32

Chapter 8: Tourism and Natural Wonders of Ethiopia 34
Introduction: 34
8.1 The Simien Mountains National Park: 34
8.2 The Danakil Depression: 34
8.3 The Rift Valley Lakes: 34
8.4 Historical and Cultural Sites: 35
8.5 Cultural Experiences: 35
8.6 Sustainable Tourism and Community Development: 35
Conclusion: 35

Chapter 9: Sustainable Development and Environmental Conservation 36
Introduction: 36

- 9.1 Environmental Challenges: 36
- 9.2 Afforestation and Reforestation: 36
- 9.3 Renewable Energy Development: 36
- 9.4 Conservation of Biodiversity: 37
- 9.5 Climate Change Adaptation: 37
- 9.6 Community-Based Conservation and Sustainable Livelihoods: 37
- Conclusion: 37

Chapter 10: Ethiopia's Role in Regional Politics and Global Diplomacy 38
- Introduction: 38
- 10.1 Historical Diplomatic Relations: 38
- 10.2 Peacekeeping and Conflict Resolution: 38
- 10.3 Mediation and Conflict Resolution: 38
- 10.4 Regional Integration and Cooperation: 39
- 10.5 Global Partnerships and Economic Diplomacy: 39
- 10.6 Climate Change and Environmental Diplomacy: 39
- Conclusion: 39

Chapter 11: Ethiopian Diaspora and Global Influence 40
- Introduction: 40
- 11.1 Historical Context of the Ethiopian Diaspora: 40
- 11.2 Cultural and Artistic Contributions: 40
- 11.3 Economic Contributions: 40
- 11.4 Political Activism and Advocacy: 40
- 11.5 Philanthropy and Development Initiatives: 41
- 11.6 Transnational Identities and Connections: 41
- 11.7 Challenges and Opportunities: 41
- Conclusion: 41

Chapter 12: Future Prospects and Emerging Trends 42
- Introduction: 42
- 12.1 Economic Growth and Industrialization: 42
- 12.2 Technological Innovation and Digital Transformation: 42
- 12.3 Infrastructure Development: 42

12.4 Sustainable Agriculture and Food Security: 43
12.5 Youth Empowerment and Entrepreneurship: 43
12.6 Gender Equality and Women's Empowerment: 43
12.7 Climate Resilience and Environmental Sustainability: 43
Conclusion: 43

Chapter 13: Health and Healthcare in Ethiopia 44
Introduction: 44
13.1 Healthcare System and Infrastructure: 44
13.2 Disease Burden and Public Health Challenges: 44
13.3 Maternal and Child Health: 44
13.4 Healthcare Workforce and Training: 45
13.5 Traditional Medicine and Integrative Healthcare: 45
13.6 Global Health Partnerships and Collaborations: 45
13.7 Health Research and Innovation: 45
Conclusion: 45

Chapter 14: Education and Human Capital Development 46
Introduction: 46
14.1 Education System Overview: 46
14.3 Quality of Education: 46
14.4 Technical and Vocational Education and Training (TVET): 47
14.5 Higher Education and Research: 47
14.6 Education for Sustainable Development: 47
14.7 Lifelong Learning and Adult Education: 47
Conclusion: 47

Chapter 15: Tourism and Cultural Heritage 48
Introduction: 48
15.1 Tourism Potential and Attractions: 48
15.2 Cultural Heritage Preservation: 48
15.3 Ecotourism and Wildlife Conservation: 48
15.4 Community-Based Tourism: 49
15.5 Tourism Infrastructure and Services: 49

15.6 Cultural Festivals and Events: 49

15.7 Tourism Marketing and Promotion: 49

Conclusion: 49

Chapter 16: Infrastructure Development and Connectivity 50

Introduction: 50

16.1 Transportation Infrastructure: 50

16.2 Energy and Power Infrastructure: 50

16.3 Water Resource Management: 50

16.4 Digital Connectivity and Telecommunications: 51

16.5 Urban Planning and Smart Cities: 51

16.6 Special Economic Zones and Industrial Parks: 51

16.7 Regional Integration and Cross-Border Infrastructure: 51

Conclusion: 51

Chapter 17: Environmental Conservation and Climate Change Mitigation 52

Introduction: 52

17.1 Biodiversity and Conservation: 52

17.2 Forest Conservation and Reforestation: 52

17.3 Sustainable Agriculture and Land Management: 52

17.4 Water Resource Management and Conservation: 53

17.5 Renewable Energy and Climate Change Mitigation: 53

17.6 Climate Change Adaptation: 53

17.7 Environmental Education and Awareness: 53

Conclusion: 53

Chapter 18: Healthcare and Public Health 54

Introduction: 54

18.1 Healthcare System Overview: 54

18.2 Healthcare Infrastructure and Facilities: 54

18.3 Primary Healthcare and Community Health: 54

18.4 Disease Prevention and Control: 54

18.5 Maternal and Child Health: 55

18.6 Non-Communicable Diseases and Chronic Care: 55

18.7 Health Information Systems and Technology: 55
18.8 Healthcare Workforce Development: 55
Conclusion: 55
Chapter 19: Exploring Ethiopian Cuisine: Flavors and Culinary Traditions 56
Origins of Ethiopian Cuisine: 56
Staple Foods and Iconic Dishes: 56
The Art of Spices and Seasonings: 56
Vegetarian and Vegan Delights: 56
Coffee Culture and Ceremony: 57
Regional Culinary Traditions: 57
Modern Innovations and Fusion Cuisine: 57
Ethiopian Beverages: 57
Ethiopian Culinary Experiences: 57
Chapter 20: Ethiopian Literature and Poetry: Unveiling Words of Wisdom and Beauty 58
The Oral Tradition: 58
Ancient Texts and Religious Manuscripts: 58
Epic Poetry and Folklore: 58
Prominent Ethiopian Writers: 59
Modern Ethiopian Literature: 59
Poetry as an Expression of Ethiopian Identity: 59
Translations and Global Recognition: 59
Literary Festivals and Cultural Events: 59
Literary Education and Institutions: 59
Glossary of Terms 61
A Song 63
Credit Note 64
Frequently Asked Questions 65
DISCLAIMER 67

Introduction

Ethiopia, a land of vibrant history, rich culture, and remarkable diversity, holds a special place in the tapestry of human civilization. From its ancient origins to its modern challenges and progress, Ethiopia's story is one of resilience, innovation, and enduring traditions.

In this book, we embark on a captivating journey through the history and culture of Ethiopia, delving into its ancient civilizations, medieval dynasties, and the intriguing interactions with Portuguese explorers. We explore the country's isolation and subsequent modernization, the political struggles that shaped its destiny, and the remarkable cultural heritage that continues to thrive.

As we delve into each chapter, we will uncover the stories of great empires and influential leaders, the contributions of Ethiopia to the wider world, and the unique religious and artistic traditions that have shaped the country's identity. From the rock-hewn churches of Lalibela to the medieval castles of Gondar, from the poetic expressions of Ethiopian literature to the tantalizing flavors of Ethiopian cuisine, each aspect reveals a facet of this remarkable nation.

However, this book is not merely a historical account. It is an invitation to experience Ethiopia's soul, to feel the heartbeat of its people, and to gain a deeper understanding of the challenges and progress that define its journey into the 21st century. We will examine the country's cultural heritage, celebrate its diversity, and explore the ongoing efforts to preserve traditions and foster development.

Throughout the pages of this book, you will encounter narratives of courage and resilience, tales of artistry and craftsmanship, and glimpses into the daily lives of Ethiopians past and present. You will discover the enduring influence of Ethiopian Orthodoxy, the beauty of traditional music and dance, and the captivating landscapes that have inspired generations.

Whether you are a curious traveler, a student of history, or simply an admirer of the world's diverse cultures, this book invites you to embark on an enlightening journey through Ethiopia. Together, let us explore the origins, traditions, challenges, and triumphs that have shaped this extraordinary nation and its remarkable people.

Join me as we unravel the tapestry of Ethiopia's past and present, and discover the threads that connect us all in the shared human experience. Welcome to "A Brief History of Ethiopia: Exploring the Heart of Africa."

Chapter 1: Origins and Ancient Civilizations

Introduction:

In the heart of Africa, amidst the rugged landscapes and fertile valleys, Ethiopia has witnessed the birth of humanity and the rise of remarkable ancient civilizations. This chapter delves into the origins of Ethiopia and explores the magnificent ancient cultures that thrived within its borders.

1.1 The Cradle of Humanity:

Ethiopia holds a significant place in the annals of human history as the cradle of humanity. It is within this land that the remains of the famous hominid fossil known as Lucy, a 3.2-million-year-old Australopithecus afarensis, were discovered. The finding shed light on our evolutionary past and positioned Ethiopia as a crucial site for the study of human origins.

1.2 The Aksumite Empire:

One of the most illustrious ancient civilizations of Ethiopia was the Aksumite Empire, which flourished from the 1st to the 7th century CE. The Aksumites established a powerful kingdom and a vibrant trade network that extended from the Red Sea to the Indian Ocean. They were renowned for their mastery of architecture, commerce, and governance.

1.2.1 Rise to Power and Aksum's Golden Age:

The Aksumite Empire emerged as a prominent force through strategic alliances and military conquests. They developed advanced agricultural techniques, built monumental structures such as obelisks, and minted their own currency, the Aksumite coinage. This era is often referred to as Aksum's Golden Age.

1.2.2 Trade Routes and the Red Sea:

The strategic location of Aksum made it a hub of international trade. Its port city, Adulis, served as a gateway for the exchange of goods, connecting Africa with the Mediterranean world, Arabia, Persia, and India. Aksum's prosperity was intertwined with the maritime trade routes and the development of a flourishing mercantile economy.

1.2.3 The Enigma of the Ark of the Covenant:

According to Ethiopian tradition, the Ark of the Covenant, believed to hold the tablets inscribed with the Ten Commandments, was brought to Aksum and housed within the Church of St. Mary of Zion. The significance of this relic, shrouded in mystery and reverence, endures as a cornerstone of Ethiopian religious and cultural identity.

1.3 Lalibela and the Rock-Hewn Churches:

In the highlands of Ethiopia lies the town of Lalibela, a UNESCO World Heritage site renowned for its awe-inspiring rock-hewn churches. Constructed in the 12th century, these remarkable structures were hewed directly from solid rock, with each church meticulously carved to create intricate architectural wonders. Lalibela stands as a testament to Ethiopia's extraordinary artistic and spiritual heritage.

Conclusion:

The origins of Ethiopia are intertwined with the story of humanity itself. From the early stages of human evolution to the heights of the Aksumite Empire and the architectural marvels of Lalibela, Ethiopia's ancient civilizations have left an indelible mark on the history of Africa and the world. As we move forward in time, we shall explore the medieval dynasties and religious heritage of Ethiopia, delving deeper into the cultural tapestry that continues to shape this remarkable nation.

Chapter 2: Medieval Dynasties and Religious Heritage

Introduction:

The medieval period in Ethiopia witnessed the rise of influential dynasties and the enduring influence of religious traditions. This chapter explores the medieval dynasties that shaped Ethiopian history and the profound impact of Orthodox Christianity on Ethiopian society and culture.

2.1 The Solomonic Dynasty:

The Solomonic Dynasty, claiming lineage from the biblical King Solomon and the Queen of Sheba, played a pivotal role in Ethiopian history for over a thousand years. This dynasty is considered Ethiopia's oldest continuous ruling house, and its rulers have been known as "Negusa Nagast" or "King of Kings."

2.1.1 Legend of the Queen of Sheba:

According to Ethiopian mythology, the Queen of Sheba, a legendary figure from the Bible, embarked on a journey to visit King Solomon in Jerusalem. The meeting between the Queen of Sheba and King Solomon resulted in the birth of Menelik I, who later became the first emperor of the Solomonic Dynasty in Ethiopia.

2.1.2 The Kingdom of Axum:

The Solomonic Dynasty expanded its influence, reaching its zenith during the Kingdom of Axum. Axum became a powerful empire, incorporating vast territories and engaging in trade with the Roman Empire, India, and Arabia. The empire's adoption of Christianity in the 4th century CE marked a significant turning point in Ethiopian history.

2.2 Orthodox Christianity:

Orthodox Christianity has been a central pillar of Ethiopian society and culture since its introduction in the 4th century CE. It has profoundly influenced Ethiopian art, architecture, literature, and daily life.

2.2.1 The Ethiopian Orthodox Tewahedo Church:

The Ethiopian Orthodox Tewahedo Church is an ancient Christian denomination with deep roots in Ethiopian society. It follows a unique liturgical tradition and preserves ancient biblical manuscripts and religious practices. The Church has played a crucial role in shaping the country's religious and cultural identity.

2.2.2 Monasticism and Religious Centers:

Monasticism flourished in Ethiopia, with numerous monasteries established throughout the country. These monastic communities served as centers of learning, artistry, and spiritual retreat, contributing to the preservation of religious texts and the development of Ethiopian religious scholarship.

2.3 The Zagwe Dynasty and the Rock-Cut Churches in Lalibela:

The Zagwe Dynasty succeeded the Solomonic Dynasty and ruled Ethiopia from the 10th to the 13th century. During this period, the Zagwe rulers commissioned the construction of remarkable rock-cut churches in Lalibela, continuing Ethiopia's rich tradition of religious architecture.

2.3.1 Lalibela's Eleven Churches:

Lalibela, a town in northern Ethiopia, is home to eleven monolithic rock-cut churches that stand as a testament to human ingenuity and religious devotion. Carved entirely from solid rock, these churches are a UNESCO World Heritage site and a pilgrimage destination for Ethiopian Orthodox Christians.

Conclusion:

The medieval dynasties of Ethiopia and the influence of Orthodox Christianity have left an indelible mark on the country's history and culture. The Solomonic Dynasty's enduring rule, the introduction of Christianity, and the magnificent rock-cut churches of Lalibela bear witness to the deep intertwining of faith, governance, and artistic expression. In the next chapter, we will explore the interactions between Ethiopia and the outside world, particularly the arrival of the Portuguese and the challenges of Ethiopian isolation.

Chapter 3: Portuguese Interactions and Ethiopian Isolation

Introduction:
During the medieval period, Ethiopia's interactions with the outside world, particularly the arrival of the Portuguese, had a significant impact on its history. This chapter delves into the dynamic encounters between Ethiopia and European powers, focusing on the Portuguese influence and the subsequent era of Ethiopian isolation.

3.1 The Arrival of the Portuguese:

In the 15th century, European powers began venturing into Africa in search of new trade routes and opportunities. The Portuguese, led by explorers such as Vasco da Gama, established contact with Ethiopia in the early 16th century.

3.1.1 Jesuit Missions and Religious Encounters:

The Portuguese Jesuit missionaries arrived in Ethiopia with the aim of spreading Catholicism and establishing closer ties with the Ethiopian Orthodox Church. Their presence brought about religious discussions, debates, and attempts at religious conversion, leading to a unique blend of Catholic and Orthodox practices in Ethiopia.

3.1.2 The Introduction of Firearms:

The Portuguese also introduced firearms to Ethiopia, transforming the nature of warfare in the region. This new military technology played a crucial role in shaping Ethiopia's subsequent conflicts and power dynamics.

3.2 The Ethiopian Empire and its Resistance against European Colonization:

As European powers expanded their colonial ambitions in Africa, Ethiopia, under the rule of emperors such as Emperor Menelik II and Emperor Haile Selassie, fiercely resisted colonization.

3.2.1 Emperor Menelik II and the Battle of Adwa:

Emperor Menelik II successfully united various Ethiopian regions and modernized the country, establishing Ethiopia as a sovereign nation. In 1896, during the Battle of Adwa, Ethiopian forces decisively defeated the Italian invasion, becoming a symbol of African resistance against European colonization.

3.2.2 Emperor Haile Selassie and the League of Nations:

Emperor Haile Selassie, a revered figure both in Ethiopia and internationally, led Ethiopia during a critical period. In 1935, Ethiopia faced a second Italian invasion, and Emperor Haile Selassie appealed to the League of Nations to condemn the aggression. Though Ethiopia was eventually occupied, its resilience and the Emperor's efforts kept the spirit of independence alive.

3.3 Ethiopian Isolation:

Following the Italian occupation, Ethiopia faced a period of isolation from the international community. The country's diplomatic and economic ties were severely strained, contributing to a sense of self-reliance and a focus on internal development.

3.3.1 Internal Struggles and Political Instability:

Ethiopia experienced internal struggles and political instability during the mid-20th century. The emergence of the Derg regime led to a period of authoritarian rule, marked by repression, human rights abuses, and economic challenges.

3.3.2 The Era of Meles Zenawi and the Ethiopian People's Revolutionary Democratic Front (EPRDF):

In 1991, the Ethiopian People's Revolutionary Democratic Front (EPRDF), led by Meles Zenawi, overthrew the Derg regime. Meles Zenawi became the Prime Minister and initiated political and economic reforms that aimed to modernize Ethiopia.

Copyright Material@

Conclusion:

The arrival of the Portuguese, their interactions with Ethiopia, and the subsequent era of Ethiopian isolation have shaped the country's history in profound ways. The resistance against colonization, the battles fought, and the emergence of influential leaders underscore Ethiopia's determination to maintain its sovereignty and preserve its cultural identity. In the next chapter, we will explore Ethiopia's vibrant cultural heritage, from its cuisine and literature to its music and dance forms.

Chapter 4: Modernization and Political Struggles

Introduction:

Ethiopia's history in the modern era is characterized by a complex interplay of modernization efforts, political struggles, and societal transformations. This chapter delves into the period of modernization and the political challenges faced by the nation, highlighting key figures and events that have shaped Ethiopia's trajectory.

4.1 Emperor Haile Selassie:

Emperor Haile Selassie, also known as the "Conquering Lion of the Tribe of Judah," played a significant role in modernizing Ethiopia and asserting its presence on the global stage. His reign, spanning from 1930 to 1974, witnessed a series of reforms and transformative initiatives.

4.1.1 Modernization Efforts:

Emperor Haile Selassie implemented extensive modernization programs, including infrastructure development, educational reforms, and the establishment of modern institutions. These efforts aimed to bring Ethiopia in line with global standards and accelerate its socioeconomic progress.

4.1.2 Italian Occupation and the League of Nations:

During Emperor Haile Selassie's reign, Ethiopia faced the Italian occupation from 1936 to 1941. His impassioned plea for international support at the League of Nations brought global attention to the plight of Ethiopia and inspired the nation's resistance against colonial forces.

4.2 The Derg Regime and the Red Terror:

In 1974, a military junta known as the Derg overthrew Emperor Haile Selassie's government, leading to a period of political repression and instability. Under the leadership of Colonel

Mengistu Haile Mariam, the Derg regime implemented socialist policies and suppressed dissent through violent means, resulting in a dark period known as the Red Terror.

4.2.1 Human Rights Abuses and Famine:

The Derg regime's brutal tactics, including mass executions and forced resettlement, led to widespread human rights abuses. Additionally, a severe famine in the 1980s exacerbated by economic mismanagement and conflict further deepened the suffering of the Ethiopian people.

4.3 The Ethiopian People's Revolutionary Democratic Front (EPRDF) and Meles Zenawi:

In 1991, the EPRDF, led by Meles Zenawi, toppled the Derg regime and established a transitional government. Meles Zenawi became the Prime Minister and embarked on a journey of political and economic reforms.

4.3.1 Democratization and Ethnic Federalism:

Under the EPRDF's rule, efforts were made to introduce a more decentralized and inclusive political system through ethnic federalism. The country was divided into regional states, granting autonomy to various ethnic groups. However, this approach also sparked tensions and conflicts along ethnic lines.

4.3.2 Economic Growth and Development:

Meles Zenawi's government pursued economic policies that aimed to spur growth and development. The implementation of ambitious infrastructure projects, such as the Grand Ethiopian Renaissance Dam, and the focus on agricultural productivity contributed to Ethiopia's emergence as one of Africa's fastest-growing economies.

4.4 Challenges and Protests in the 21st Century:

In recent years, Ethiopia has faced significant challenges, including political unrest, ethnic tensions, and demands for greater democratic reforms. Protests and demonstrations by various groups have called for inclusive governance, respect for human rights, and the resolution of ethnic conflicts.

Conclusion:

Ethiopia's modern history is marked by the visionary leadership of Emperor Haile Selassie, the dark period of the Derg regime, and the subsequent political reforms initiated by the EPRDF.

The nation's journey towards modernization has been accompanied by political struggles, societal transformations, and calls for greater inclusivity and democracy. In the next chapter, we will explore Ethiopia's vibrant cultural heritage, encompassing its cuisine, literature, music, and artistic expressions, which continue to flourish amidst the challenges and changes of the modern era.

Chapter 5: Cultural Heritage and Diversity

Introduction:

Ethiopia is a tapestry of diverse cultures, traditions, and artistic expressions. This chapter delves into the rich cultural heritage of Ethiopia, encompassing its cuisine, literature, music, and artistic traditions. It explores the ways in which these cultural elements contribute to Ethiopia's unique identity and foster a sense of unity amidst its diverse population.

5.1 Ethiopian Cuisine:

Ethiopian cuisine is renowned for its vibrant flavors, unique cooking techniques, and communal dining traditions. The staple food, injera, a sourdough flatbread, serves as the foundation of many Ethiopian meals. Dishes such as doro wat (spicy chicken stew), kitfo (minced raw meat), and injera with a variety of flavorful stews showcase the country's rich culinary heritage.

5.1.1 Coffee Culture:

Ethiopia is widely regarded as the birthplace of coffee, and the country has a deeply ingrained coffee culture. The traditional Ethiopian coffee ceremony, a ritualistic and social event, involves the roasting, grinding, and brewing of coffee beans, creating a fragrant and invigorating experience for participants.

5.2 Ethiopian Literature:

Ethiopia has a long and distinguished literary tradition, with a rich collection of oral and written works. From ancient manuscripts to contemporary literature, Ethiopian writers have contributed to the nation's literary landscape. The works of prominent Ethiopian authors, such as Tsegaye Gabre-Medhin and Maaza Mengiste, offer insights into Ethiopian history, culture, and societal challenges.

5.3 Music and Dance:

Music and dance form an integral part of Ethiopian cultural expression. Traditional Ethiopian music encompasses a variety of styles, including the distinctive sounds of the masinko (a single-stringed bowed instrument) and the hypnotic rhythms of the kebero (a traditional drum). Ethiopian traditional dances, such as the eskista, showcase intricate movements and vibrant costumes, captivating audiences with their energy and grace.

5.4 Artistic Traditions:

Ethiopia boasts a rich artistic heritage, with diverse artistic traditions across the country. From ancient rock art in places like Tigray and Afar regions to the intricate religious paintings found in Ethiopian Orthodox churches, art serves as a medium to convey religious, historical, and cultural narratives. Contemporary Ethiopian artists, such as Elias Sime and Aida Muluneh, have gained international recognition for their innovative and thought-provoking works.

5.5 Cultural Festivals and Celebrations:

Ethiopia is home to a myriad of cultural festivals and celebrations that reflect the country's religious and ethnic diversity. Timkat, the Ethiopian Orthodox Epiphany celebration, is a colorful and vibrant festival that involves processions, baptismal rituals, and feasting. Other festivals, such as Meskel (Finding of the True Cross) and Irreecha (Oromo Thanksgiving), provide opportunities for communities to come together, celebrate, and honor their cultural heritage.

Conclusion:

Ethiopia's cultural heritage is a testament to its diversity, resilience, and the rich tapestry of its people. From its distinctive cuisine and literary traditions to the captivating music, dance, and visual arts, Ethiopia's cultural expressions reflect the nation's history, beliefs, and values. Embracing its cultural diversity, Ethiopia continues to celebrate and preserve its heritage, nurturing a sense of unity and pride among its people. In the next chapter, we will explore the natural wonders and breathtaking landscapes that make Ethiopia a truly remarkable country.

Chapter 6: Challenges and Progress in the 21st Century

Introduction:

The 21st century has presented Ethiopia with a unique set of challenges and opportunities. This chapter examines the key issues and notable advancements that have shaped the country in recent years, ranging from economic development and infrastructure projects to social and political challenges.

6.1 Economic Growth and Development:

Ethiopia has experienced significant economic growth and development in the 21st century. The government has implemented ambitious plans, such as the Growth and Transformation Plan (GTP) and the current Ethiopian Vision 2025, aimed at promoting industrialization, improving infrastructure, and reducing poverty. The country has attracted foreign investment and witnessed the emergence of various industries, contributing to its economic transformation.

6.1.1 Infrastructure Development:

Ethiopia has invested heavily in infrastructure projects, including the construction of roads, railways, dams, and industrial parks. The Grand Ethiopian Renaissance Dam, one of the largest hydroelectric projects in Africa, has the potential to provide abundant energy and transform the country's power generation capacity.

6.2 Social and Political Challenges:

Despite the progress made, Ethiopia continues to face significant social and political challenges that require attention and resolution.

6.2.1 Ethnic Tensions and Conflicts:

Ethnic tensions and conflicts have emerged as a major challenge in Ethiopia. The country's diverse ethnic makeup, coupled with historical grievances and competition for resources, has resulted in sporadic outbreaks of violence and displacement of communities. Addressing these tensions and promoting inclusive governance are crucial for ensuring peace and stability.

6.2.2 Human Rights and Press Freedom:

Human rights concerns, including restrictions on freedom of expression and assembly, have been raised by international observers and advocacy groups. Balancing security concerns with the protection of individual rights remains a critical task for Ethiopia's government.

6.3 Democratic Reforms:

In recent years, Ethiopia has witnessed significant political reforms aimed at promoting democratic governance and inclusivity. The appointment of Abiy Ahmed as Prime Minister in 2018 marked a turning point, leading to a series of reforms such as the release of political prisoners, the opening of political space, and the initiation of dialogue with opposition groups.

6.3.1 The Nobel Peace Prize and Regional Diplomacy:

In 2019, Prime Minister Abiy Ahmed was awarded the Nobel Peace Prize for his efforts to resolve the long-standing conflict between Ethiopia and Eritrea, demonstrating Ethiopia's commitment to regional peace and stability.

6.4 Environmental Conservation and Climate Change:

Ethiopia is vulnerable to the impacts of climate change, including droughts, desertification, and water scarcity. The country has undertaken various initiatives to mitigate these effects and promote environmental conservation. The Green Legacy Initiative, spearheaded by Prime Minister Abiy Ahmed, aims to combat deforestation and promote reforestation efforts.

6.4.1 Sustainable Agriculture and Food Security:

Ethiopia is actively working towards achieving sustainable agriculture practices and enhancing food security. Initiatives focused on improving agricultural productivity, enhancing irrigation systems, and supporting smallholder farmers have been implemented to address the challenges of food insecurity.

Conclusion:

The 21st century has brought both progress and challenges for Ethiopia. The country's focus on economic development, infrastructure projects, and democratic reforms has set the stage for a transformative future. However, social and political challenges, including ethnic tensions and human rights concerns, need to be addressed to ensure stability and inclusivity. Ethiopia's commitment to environmental conservation and sustainable development exemplifies its dedication to creating a more resilient and prosperous future. As Ethiopia continues to navigate these complexities, its resilience and determination to overcome challenges will shape its path forward.

Chapter 7: Education and Human Development

Introduction:

Education and human development play a crucial role in shaping the progress and future of Ethiopia. This chapter explores the evolution of education in Ethiopia, its challenges, and the efforts made to improve access to quality education and enhance human development across the country.

7.1 Historical Overview of Education in Ethiopia:

Education has a long history in Ethiopia, with early institutions focused primarily on religious education. The Ethiopian Orthodox Church played a significant role in the preservation and dissemination of knowledge. The chapter explores the traditional educational systems and the challenges faced in expanding access to education throughout the centuries.

7.2 Challenges in Education:

Ethiopia faces numerous challenges in its education system, including limited access to schooling, inadequate infrastructure, teacher shortages, and gender disparities. This section examines the barriers that have hindered the educational progress in the country.

7.2.1 Access to Education:

Ethiopia has made efforts to improve access to education, but significant gaps still exist, especially in rural areas. Factors such as poverty, distance to schools, cultural norms, and the impact of conflicts and displacement have limited educational opportunities for many Ethiopian children.

7.2.2 Quality of Education:

Ensuring quality education remains a challenge in Ethiopia. This section discusses issues such as a shortage of trained teachers, outdated teaching methods, inadequate learning materials, and the need for curriculum reforms to meet the demands of a rapidly changing world.

7.3 Government Initiatives and Reforms:

The Ethiopian government has implemented various initiatives and reforms to address the challenges in education and promote human development.

7.3.1 Universal Primary Education:

The government has prioritized achieving universal primary education, aiming to ensure that all children have access to and complete a basic education. Efforts to eliminate school fees, increase school construction, and improve teacher training have been implemented to enhance primary education in Ethiopia.

7.3.2 Technical and Vocational Education and Training (TVET):

Recognizing the importance of skills development, the Ethiopian government has invested in expanding TVET programs to provide students with practical skills that align with the needs of the job market. This section explores the growth of TVET institutions and their impact on youth employment and economic development.

7.4 Higher Education and Research:

Ethiopia has made significant progress in expanding higher education opportunities and investing in research and innovation. The establishment of universities, research centers, and scholarship programs has contributed to the development of a knowledgeable workforce and the advancement of scientific research in various fields.

7.5 Women's Empowerment and Gender Equality:

Promoting gender equality in education is a crucial aspect of human development in Ethiopia. This section discusses the efforts made to address gender disparities, increase girls' enrollment, and empower women through education and skills training.

Conclusion:

Education and human development are essential pillars for Ethiopia's progress and future prosperity. Despite the challenges, the country has demonstrated a commitment to expanding access to education, improving quality, and empowering its citizens. By investing in education and fostering human development, Ethiopia is laying the foundation for a brighter and more inclusive society, where individuals can realize their full potential and contribute to the nation's growth. In the next chapter, we will explore Ethiopia's natural wonders and its significance as a tourist destination.

Chapter 8: Tourism and Natural Wonders of Ethiopia

Introduction:

Ethiopia is a land of stunning natural beauty and diverse landscapes, making it a captivating destination for travelers. This chapter explores the country's natural wonders, cultural attractions, and the growing tourism industry, shedding light on Ethiopia's unique appeal and its potential as a tourist destination.

8.1 The Simien Mountains National Park:

The Simien Mountains, a UNESCO World Heritage site, offer breathtaking scenery and unique wildlife. This section highlights the park's dramatic peaks, deep valleys, and endemic species such as the Ethiopian wolf and the Gelada baboon, attracting nature enthusiasts and hikers from around the world.

8.2 The Danakil Depression:

The Danakil Depression, one of the hottest and lowest places on Earth, provides a surreal and otherworldly experience. This chapter explores the region's colorful sulfur springs, salt flats, lava lakes, and the active volcano Erta Ale, offering a glimpse into the raw power of nature.

8.3 The Rift Valley Lakes:

Ethiopia's Great Rift Valley is home to a series of stunning lakes, each with its unique features and attractions. This section explores the beautiful Lake Tana, the largest lake in Ethiopia and the source of the Blue Nile, as well as Lake Abiyata-Shala, known for its birdlife and the presence of hot springs.

8.4 Historical and Cultural Sites:

Ethiopia is renowned for its ancient historical and cultural sites, which offer a glimpse into the country's rich heritage. This chapter highlights iconic attractions such as the rock-hewn churches of Lalibela, the ancient city of Aksum with its obelisks and ruins, and the medieval castles of Gondar, showcasing Ethiopia's architectural and historical treasures.

8.5 Cultural Experiences:

Ethiopia's cultural diversity and vibrant traditions provide immersive experiences for visitors. This section explores the vibrant markets of Addis Ababa, where one can explore traditional crafts and sample local cuisine. The chapter also delves into cultural festivals, such as the colorful celebration of Timkat and the mesmerizing music and dance performances that showcase Ethiopia's rich artistic heritage.

8.6 Sustainable Tourism and Community Development:

As the tourism industry grows in Ethiopia, efforts are being made to promote sustainable practices and community development. This section discusses initiatives that focus on preserving natural and cultural heritage, supporting local communities, and providing authentic and responsible travel experiences.

Conclusion:

Ethiopia's natural wonders, cultural attractions, and historical sites offer a unique and enriching experience for travelers. From its majestic mountains and stunning lakes to its ancient churches and vibrant traditions, Ethiopia has much to offer to those seeking adventure, cultural immersion, and natural beauty. As the tourism industry continues to grow, it is essential to ensure that sustainable practices are embraced to protect Ethiopia's natural and cultural heritage for future generations. By showcasing its natural wonders and rich cultural tapestry, Ethiopia is poised to become a leading destination for global travelers.

Chapter 9: Sustainable Development and Environmental Conservation

Introduction:

Ethiopia has recognized the importance of sustainable development and environmental conservation in securing a prosperous and resilient future. This chapter explores the country's efforts to promote sustainable practices, protect its natural resources, and mitigate the effects of climate change.

9.1 Environmental Challenges:

Ethiopia faces a range of environmental challenges, including deforestation, soil erosion, desertification, and water scarcity. This section discusses the causes and consequences of these challenges, emphasizing the need for urgent action to safeguard the country's ecosystems.

9.2 Afforestation and Reforestation:

Ethiopia has launched ambitious afforestation and reforestation initiatives to combat deforestation and restore degraded landscapes. The chapter explores programs such as the Green Legacy Initiative and the Sustainable Land Management Program, which aim to increase forest cover, improve soil quality, and promote sustainable land use practices.

9.3 Renewable Energy Development:

Ethiopia has significant potential for renewable energy, particularly hydropower, wind, and solar. This section highlights the country's efforts to harness its renewable energy resources, reduce dependence on fossil fuels, and promote clean and sustainable energy production.

9.4 Conservation of Biodiversity:

Ethiopia is known for its rich biodiversity, with numerous endemic species and unique ecosystems. This chapter discusses the country's efforts to protect its biodiversity through the establishment of national parks, wildlife sanctuaries, and conservation programs. It also explores the importance of preserving critical habitats and promoting sustainable wildlife management.

9.5 Climate Change Adaptation:

Ethiopia is particularly vulnerable to the impacts of climate change, including increased frequency and intensity of droughts, unpredictable rainfall patterns, and rising temperatures. This section explores the country's strategies for climate change adaptation, including water management, sustainable agriculture practices, and early warning systems for natural disasters.

9.6 Community-Based Conservation and Sustainable Livelihoods:

Ethiopia recognizes the importance of involving local communities in conservation efforts and ensuring that they benefit from sustainable practices. This chapter discusses community-based conservation initiatives, sustainable livelihood projects, and the integration of indigenous knowledge in natural resource management.

Conclusion:

Ethiopia's commitment to sustainable development and environmental conservation reflects its determination to safeguard its natural resources and build a resilient future. By addressing environmental challenges, promoting renewable energy, conserving biodiversity, and engaging local communities, Ethiopia is positioning itself as a leader in sustainable practices. Through these efforts, the country aims to ensure the well-being of its people, protect its unique ecosystems, and contribute to global efforts to mitigate climate change. In the next chapter, we will examine Ethiopia's role in regional politics and its contributions to peacekeeping and diplomacy.

Chapter 10: Ethiopia's Role in Regional Politics and Global Diplomacy

Introduction:

Ethiopia has played a significant role in regional politics and global diplomacy, actively participating in peacekeeping efforts and engaging in diplomatic relations with nations around the world. This chapter explores Ethiopia's diplomatic history, its contributions to regional stability, and its involvement in international affairs.

10.1 Historical Diplomatic Relations:

Ethiopia has a long history of diplomatic relations with various nations. This section highlights the country's historical connections with neighboring countries, as well as its engagement with major powers and international organizations throughout different periods.

10.2 Peacekeeping and Conflict Resolution:

Ethiopia has been an active participant in peacekeeping missions, contributing troops and resources to promote peace and stability in conflict-affected regions. This chapter examines Ethiopia's involvement in peacekeeping efforts in places such as South Sudan, Somalia, and the African Union Mission in Darfur, showcasing its commitment to regional security.

10.3 Mediation and Conflict Resolution:

Ethiopia has also played a crucial role in mediating conflicts and facilitating peace processes. The section discusses Ethiopia's efforts in mediating regional disputes, such as the peace talks between South Sudanese factions and its role in the Ethiopian-Eritrean peace agreement, which led to the normalization of relations between the two countries.

10.4 Regional Integration and Cooperation:

Ethiopia has actively participated in regional organizations and initiatives aimed at promoting economic integration and cooperation. This chapter explores Ethiopia's involvement in organizations such as the African Union (AU), the Intergovernmental Authority on Development (IGAD), and the East African Community (EAC), highlighting its contributions to regional development and collaboration.

10.5 Global Partnerships and Economic Diplomacy:

Ethiopia has sought to strengthen its global partnerships and attract foreign investment through economic diplomacy. This section discusses Ethiopia's efforts to foster trade and investment relations with countries such as China, the United States, and European nations, and explores the impact of these partnerships on Ethiopia's economic development.

10.6 Climate Change and Environmental Diplomacy:

Ethiopia has been an active participant in global discussions on climate change and environmental sustainability. This chapter examines Ethiopia's role in international climate negotiations, its commitment to renewable energy, and its efforts to advocate for climate justice and sustainable development on the global stage.

Conclusion:

Ethiopia's active engagement in regional politics and global diplomacy demonstrates its commitment to peace, stability, and international cooperation. Through its participation in peacekeeping missions, mediation efforts, and regional integration initiatives, Ethiopia has contributed significantly to regional stability. Moreover, its involvement in global partnerships and environmental diplomacy highlights its dedication to addressing pressing global challenges. As Ethiopia continues to play an active role in international affairs, its diplomatic engagements will shape its position as a regional leader and a respected global player.

Chapter 11: Ethiopian Diaspora and Global Influence

Introduction:

The Ethiopian diaspora has spread across the globe, with significant communities residing in various countries. This chapter explores the influence of the Ethiopian diaspora, their contributions to their host nations and Ethiopia, and their role in shaping global perceptions of Ethiopian culture, politics, and development.

11.1 Historical Context of the Ethiopian Diaspora:

The Ethiopian diaspora has roots in different periods of history, including political upheavals, economic opportunities, and educational pursuits. This section provides an overview of the historical context that led to the dispersion of Ethiopians around the world.

11.2 Cultural and Artistic Contributions:

Ethiopian diaspora communities have played a crucial role in preserving and promoting Ethiopian culture and heritage. This chapter examines their contributions to music, art, literature, and cuisine, showcasing how the diaspora has enriched the global cultural landscape.

11.3 Economic Contributions:

The Ethiopian diaspora has made significant economic contributions both in their host countries and in Ethiopia. This section explores the entrepreneurial ventures, investments, and remittances sent back home, which have helped stimulate economic growth and development in Ethiopia.

11.4 Political Activism and Advocacy:

Ethiopian diaspora communities have been active in political activism and advocacy, advocating for human rights, democracy, and justice in Ethiopia. This chapter delves into their efforts to raise awareness, organize protests, and engage in lobbying activities to influence policy and bring attention to key issues affecting Ethiopia.

11.5 Philanthropy and Development Initiatives:

The Ethiopian diaspora has initiated numerous philanthropic and development projects, aiming to improve the lives of people in Ethiopia. This section highlights their contributions to education, healthcare, infrastructure development, and poverty alleviation, showcasing their commitment to supporting their home country.

11.6 Transnational Identities and Connections:

The Ethiopian diaspora has maintained strong connections with their Ethiopian roots while adapting to their new cultural environments. This chapter explores the formation of transnational identities, the fostering of cross-cultural exchanges, and the role of diaspora networks in fostering cooperation and collaboration.

11.7 Challenges and Opportunities:

The Ethiopian diaspora faces various challenges, including cultural assimilation, discrimination, and the complexities of navigating dual identities. This section also highlights the opportunities for collaboration between the diaspora and Ethiopia, such as knowledge transfer, investment, and fostering partnerships for sustainable development.

Conclusion:

The Ethiopian diaspora has had a profound impact on the global stage, influencing cultural expressions, advocating for political change, and contributing to economic development. Their contributions have helped shape global perceptions of Ethiopia and fostered a sense of pride and connection among Ethiopians around the world. As the diaspora continues to engage and collaborate, their collective efforts have the potential to further strengthen Ethiopia's global influence and contribute to the country's progress and prosperity.

Chapter 12: Future Prospects and Emerging Trends

Introduction:

As Ethiopia moves forward, several emerging trends and future prospects are shaping the country's trajectory. This chapter explores key areas of development, technological advancements, and social changes that hold significant potential for Ethiopia's future growth and prosperity.

12.1 Economic Growth and Industrialization:

Ethiopia has been experiencing robust economic growth and aims to become a middle-income country in the coming years. This section examines the government's efforts to promote industrialization, expand manufacturing sectors, and attract foreign investment to drive economic diversification and job creation.

12.2 Technological Innovation and Digital Transformation:

Ethiopia has recognized the transformative power of technology and is embracing digital transformation. This chapter explores the growth of the technology sector, the rise of tech startups, and the government's initiatives to promote digital connectivity, e-commerce, and digital skills development.

12.3 Infrastructure Development:

Investments in infrastructure development, such as transportation, energy, and telecommunications, are crucial for Ethiopia's progress. This section discusses ongoing infrastructure projects, including the construction of roads, railways, and power plants, and their potential to enhance connectivity, stimulate economic growth, and improve the quality of life for Ethiopians.

12.4 Sustainable Agriculture and Food Security:

Agriculture remains a vital sector in Ethiopia, employing a significant portion of the population. This chapter explores the country's efforts to promote sustainable agricultural practices, enhance productivity, and ensure food security through initiatives such as irrigation systems, improved seed varieties, and climate-smart agriculture.

12.5 Youth Empowerment and Entrepreneurship:

Ethiopia has a young and vibrant population, presenting both opportunities and challenges. This section discusses the government's focus on youth empowerment, skills development, and entrepreneurship to harness the potential of the youth demographic and drive innovation and economic growth.

12.6 Gender Equality and Women's Empowerment:

Promoting gender equality and women's empowerment is essential for Ethiopia's sustainable development. This chapter examines the government's efforts to enhance women's access to education, healthcare, and economic opportunities, as well as address gender-based violence and discrimination.

12.7 Climate Resilience and Environmental Sustainability:

Ethiopia is highly vulnerable to the impacts of climate change. This section explores the country's strategies for climate resilience, including reforestation programs, renewable energy investments, and climate adaptation measures, to mitigate the adverse effects and build a more sustainable and resilient future.

Conclusion:

Ethiopia's future prospects are promising, with opportunities for economic growth, technological advancements, and social progress. By focusing on industrialization, innovation, sustainable development, and empowering its youth and women, Ethiopia can unlock its full potential and achieve its vision of a prosperous and inclusive nation. It is crucial to address challenges, such as climate change, infrastructure gaps, and social inequalities, to ensure a sustainable and equitable future for all Ethiopians. As Ethiopia continues to embrace emerging trends and navigate its path forward, it has the potential to become a model for development and a regional leader in various sectors.

Chapter 13: Health and Healthcare in Ethiopia

Introduction:

The health sector plays a vital role in Ethiopia's development and the well-being of its population. This chapter explores the healthcare system, public health initiatives, and the challenges and progress in improving health outcomes for Ethiopians.

13.1 Healthcare System and Infrastructure:

The healthcare system in Ethiopia consists of various levels, from primary healthcare centers to specialized hospitals. This section provides an overview of the healthcare infrastructure, including the distribution of healthcare facilities and the accessibility of healthcare services in urban and rural areas.

13.2 Disease Burden and Public Health Challenges:

Ethiopia faces significant health challenges, including high rates of communicable diseases such as malaria, tuberculosis, and HIV/AIDS, as well as non-communicable diseases like cardiovascular diseases and diabetes. This chapter examines the disease burden and the efforts to address public health challenges through preventive measures, vaccination programs, and disease control initiatives.

13.3 Maternal and Child Health:

Maternal and child health is a critical area of focus in Ethiopia. This section explores the initiatives aimed at reducing maternal and infant mortality rates, improving access to antenatal and postnatal care, promoting family planning, and enhancing nutrition and immunization programs for children.

13.4 Healthcare Workforce and Training:

Ensuring an adequate and skilled healthcare workforce is crucial for delivering quality healthcare services. This chapter discusses the training and capacity-building efforts in the healthcare sector, including medical education, nursing programs, and the recruitment and retention of healthcare professionals.

13.5 Traditional Medicine and Integrative Healthcare:

Traditional medicine has long been a part of Ethiopian culture and healthcare practices. This section explores the integration of traditional medicine with modern healthcare systems, the regulation of traditional medicine practitioners, and the efforts to preserve traditional healing practices.

13.6 Global Health Partnerships and Collaborations:

Ethiopia has been a partner in various global health initiatives, working with international organizations, non-governmental organizations, and donor agencies to address health challenges. This chapter examines the collaborations, funding, and knowledge sharing in areas such as disease control, maternal and child health, and health system strengthening.

13.7 Health Research and Innovation:

Research and innovation are essential for advancing healthcare practices and addressing health challenges. This section discusses the research efforts in Ethiopia, including medical research institutions, partnerships with international research organizations, and the promotion of innovation in healthcare delivery.

Conclusion:

Health and healthcare are critical components of Ethiopia's development agenda. By addressing public health challenges, improving healthcare infrastructure, and strengthening the healthcare workforce, Ethiopia can make significant strides in improving the well-being of its population. Collaboration with global health partners, investments in research and innovation, and a focus on preventive healthcare and community-based interventions will contribute to achieving sustainable improvements in health outcomes for Ethiopians. As Ethiopia continues to prioritize health, it has the potential to become a model for healthcare advancements and make substantial progress in achieving universal health coverage and improving the overall quality of life for its citizens.

Chapter 14: Education and Human Capital Development

Introduction:

Education is a crucial foundation for human capital development and socio-economic progress. This chapter explores Ethiopia's education system, initiatives to improve access and quality of education, and the role of education in shaping the country's future.

14.1 Education System Overview:

This section provides an overview of Ethiopia's education system, including primary, secondary, and tertiary education. It examines the structure, curriculum, and enrollment rates, highlighting both the achievements and challenges in providing quality education to all Ethiopians.

14.2 Access to Education:

Access to education has been a significant focus in Ethiopia's development efforts. This chapter discusses initiatives to improve access, including the expansion of school infrastructure, community-based schools, and efforts to address gender disparities and ensure education for marginalized populations.

14.3 Quality of Education:

Ensuring quality education is essential for human capital development. This section explores the efforts to enhance the quality of education, including curriculum reforms, teacher training programs, and the integration of technology in classrooms. It also examines challenges such as overcrowded classrooms and the need for ongoing teacher professional development.

14.4 Technical and Vocational Education and Training (TVET):

TVET plays a vital role in equipping individuals with practical skills and preparing them for the workforce. This chapter discusses the expansion of TVET programs, public-private partnerships in skills development, and efforts to align TVET with industry needs to enhance employability.

14.5 Higher Education and Research:

Higher education institutions are critical for fostering innovation, research, and producing a skilled workforce. This section explores the development of universities, research institutes, and centers of excellence in Ethiopia, highlighting their contributions to knowledge generation, technological advancements, and human capital development.

14.6 Education for Sustainable Development:

Promoting education for sustainable development is essential for Ethiopia's long-term sustainability. This chapter examines initiatives to incorporate environmental awareness, climate change education, and sustainable practices into the education system, fostering a culture of environmental stewardship and sustainable development.

14.7 Lifelong Learning and Adult Education:

Lifelong learning and adult education programs are essential for continuous skills development and addressing literacy gaps. This section explores adult literacy programs, non-formal education initiatives, and opportunities for adults to acquire new skills and enhance their livelihoods.

Conclusion:

Education is a powerful catalyst for Ethiopia's development, empowering individuals, driving innovation, and fostering social and economic progress. By addressing the challenges of access, quality, and relevance, Ethiopia can harness the full potential of its human capital and build a knowledge-based society. Investment in education, collaboration with international partners, and a focus on inclusive and equitable education will lay the foundation for Ethiopia's future success. As Ethiopia continues to prioritize education and human capital development, it will unlock opportunities for individuals, contribute to sustainable development, and shape a brighter future for the nation.

Chapter 15: Tourism and Cultural Heritage

Introduction:

Ethiopia is a land of rich cultural heritage, breathtaking landscapes, and historical treasures. This chapter explores the potential of tourism as a driver of economic growth, the preservation of cultural heritage sites, and the promotion of Ethiopia as a tourist destination.

15.1 Tourism Potential and Attractions:

Ethiopia boasts a diverse range of tourist attractions, including ancient historical sites, stunning natural landscapes, vibrant cultural festivals, and unique wildlife. This section highlights the country's tourism potential, showcasing popular destinations such as Lalibela, Axum, the Simien Mountains, the Omo Valley, and Lake Tana.

15.2 Cultural Heritage Preservation:

Preserving Ethiopia's cultural heritage is vital for promoting sustainable tourism and safeguarding the country's unique identity. This chapter discusses efforts to protect and restore historical sites, ancient artifacts, traditional crafts, and intangible cultural heritage, ensuring their preservation for future generations.

15.3 Ecotourism and Wildlife Conservation:

Ethiopia's diverse ecosystems, national parks, and wildlife reserves offer significant opportunities for ecotourism and wildlife conservation. This section explores initiatives to promote responsible tourism practices, protect endangered species, and preserve natural habitats, striking a balance between tourism and environmental sustainability.

15.4 Community-Based Tourism:

Community-based tourism initiatives empower local communities by involving them in tourism activities and sharing the benefits of tourism revenue. This chapter examines community-based tourism projects, homestays, and cultural immersion experiences, fostering cultural exchange, and supporting local livelihoods.

15.5 Tourism Infrastructure and Services:

Developing tourism infrastructure and services is crucial for attracting visitors and enhancing the tourism experience. This section discusses the improvement of transportation networks, accommodation options, tour guide training, and visitor services to ensure a positive and memorable tourist experience in Ethiopia.

15.6 Cultural Festivals and Events:

Ethiopia's vibrant cultural festivals and events showcase the country's rich traditions, music, dance, and religious celebrations. This chapter explores the significance of festivals such as Timkat, Meskel, and Enkutatash, and their potential to attract domestic and international tourists, promoting cultural exchange and tourism development.

15.7 Tourism Marketing and Promotion:

Efficient marketing and promotion strategies are essential for attracting tourists to Ethiopia. This section examines the government's efforts to market Ethiopia as a tourist destination, including destination branding, digital marketing campaigns, participation in international tourism fairs, and collaborations with tour operators and travel agencies.

Conclusion:

Tourism presents a significant opportunity for Ethiopia's economic growth, job creation, and cultural preservation. By capitalizing on its unique attractions, preserving cultural heritage, and implementing sustainable tourism practices, Ethiopia can position itself as a top tourist destination. However, it is essential to balance tourism development with environmental conservation, community involvement, and the preservation of cultural authenticity. Through strategic marketing, infrastructure development, and capacity building, Ethiopia can harness the transformative power of tourism and create a sustainable tourism industry that benefits local communities, protects natural resources, and showcases Ethiopia's rich cultural heritage to the world.

Chapter 16: Infrastructure Development and Connectivity

Introduction:

Infrastructure development is crucial for Ethiopia's economic growth, regional integration, and social progress. This chapter explores the country's efforts to improve infrastructure, enhance connectivity, and foster economic development through the development of transportation networks, energy systems, and digital connectivity.

16.1 Transportation Infrastructure:

Efficient transportation infrastructure is vital for connecting communities, facilitating trade, and supporting economic growth. This section examines the development of road networks, railways, airports, and seaports in Ethiopia, highlighting the role of infrastructure in improving mobility, logistics, and regional integration.

16.2 Energy and Power Infrastructure:

Access to reliable and affordable energy is essential for powering industries, households, and driving economic development. This chapter discusses Ethiopia's energy infrastructure, including hydroelectric power plants, wind farms, and geothermal energy projects, as well as initiatives to promote renewable energy and expand access to electricity in rural areas.

16.3 Water Resource Management:

Effective water resource management is crucial for agriculture, hydroelectric power generation, and ensuring water availability for communities. This section explores Ethiopia's efforts in building dams, reservoirs, and irrigation systems to manage water resources, promote sustainable water usage, and mitigate the impacts of climate change.

16.4 Digital Connectivity and Telecommunications:

In the digital age, access to reliable internet connectivity is essential for social inclusion, education, e-commerce, and communication. This chapter examines Ethiopia's efforts to expand digital connectivity, develop broadband infrastructure, and promote e-governance and digital literacy to bridge the digital divide and drive digital transformation.

16.5 Urban Planning and Smart Cities:

As urbanization accelerates, effective urban planning is critical for sustainable and livable cities. This section explores Ethiopia's urban development initiatives, including the creation of smart cities, affordable housing projects, and efforts to improve urban infrastructure, transportation, and waste management systems.

16.6 Special Economic Zones and Industrial Parks:

Special economic zones and industrial parks are important drivers of economic growth and foreign direct investment. This chapter discusses Ethiopia's development of special economic zones and industrial parks, attracting domestic and international investments, creating job opportunities, and promoting exports.

16.7 Regional Integration and Cross-Border Infrastructure:

Ethiopia's geographical location presents opportunities for regional integration and cross-border infrastructure development. This section explores initiatives to enhance connectivity with neighboring countries, such as road and rail links, power interconnections, and regional trade agreements, fostering economic cooperation and integration.

Conclusion:

Infrastructure development and connectivity are vital components of Ethiopia's development agenda. By investing in transportation networks, energy systems, digital connectivity, and water resource management, Ethiopia can enhance economic competitiveness, improve living standards, and promote regional integration. It is crucial to prioritize sustainable and inclusive infrastructure development, ensuring that infrastructure projects benefit all segments of society and contribute to Ethiopia's long-term sustainability and resilience. As Ethiopia continues to advance its infrastructure agenda, it will unlock new economic opportunities, improve access to essential services, and create a foundation for a prosperous and connected future.

Chapter 17: Environmental Conservation and Climate Change Mitigation

Introduction:

Ethiopia is blessed with diverse ecosystems, but it also faces environmental challenges such as deforestation, soil erosion, and climate change impacts. This chapter explores Ethiopia's efforts to conserve its natural resources, mitigate climate change, and promote sustainable environmental practices.

17.1 Biodiversity and Conservation:

Ethiopia is home to unique and diverse flora and fauna. This section discusses the country's efforts to protect and conserve its biodiversity through the establishment of national parks, wildlife reserves, and conservation initiatives. It also explores the importance of biodiversity conservation for ecosystem health and sustainable development.

17.2 Forest Conservation and Reforestation:

Deforestation poses a significant threat to Ethiopia's environment and communities. This chapter examines initiatives to combat deforestation, promote sustainable forestry practices, and implement large-scale reforestation programs like the Green Legacy Initiative, aimed at restoring degraded lands and increasing forest cover.

17.3 Sustainable Agriculture and Land Management:

Agriculture is a vital sector in Ethiopia, but unsustainable practices can lead to land degradation and reduced productivity. This section explores sustainable agricultural practices, such as agroforestry, conservation agriculture, and watershed management, promoting soil health, water conservation, and long-term agricultural sustainability.

17.4 Water Resource Management and Conservation:

Ethiopia's water resources are crucial for agriculture, energy production, and ecosystems. This chapter discusses integrated water resource management, water conservation measures, and initiatives to address water scarcity, ensuring sustainable water usage and protecting water sources from pollution and degradation.

17.5 Renewable Energy and Climate Change Mitigation:

Ethiopia is committed to reducing its greenhouse gas emissions and transitioning to a low-carbon economy. This section explores the country's efforts in renewable energy development, including hydropower, wind power, and solar energy projects, as well as initiatives to promote energy efficiency and mitigate climate change impacts.

17.6 Climate Change Adaptation:

Ethiopia is vulnerable to the impacts of climate change, including increased droughts, erratic rainfall patterns, and temperature extremes. This chapter discusses adaptation strategies, such as climate-resilient agriculture, early warning systems, and community-based climate change adaptation programs, enhancing the country's resilience to climate change.

17.7 Environmental Education and Awareness:

Promoting environmental education and awareness is crucial for fostering a culture of environmental stewardship. This section explores initiatives to raise awareness about environmental conservation, engage communities in sustainable practices, and integrate environmental education into the formal education system.

Conclusion:

Ethiopia's commitment to environmental conservation and climate change mitigation is essential for sustainable development and the well-being of its people. By implementing effective conservation strategies, promoting sustainable land and water management, investing in renewable energy, and raising environmental awareness, Ethiopia can protect its natural resources, mitigate climate change impacts, and build a resilient and sustainable future. Collaboration with International partners, innovative approaches to environmental conservation, and the active participation of local communities are key to achieving Ethiopia's environmental goals and ensuring a sustainable and healthy environment for generations to come.

Chapter 18: Healthcare and Public Health

Introduction:

Access to quality healthcare is crucial for the well-being of Ethiopia's population and the overall development of the country. This chapter explores Ethiopia's healthcare system, efforts to improve healthcare access, address public health challenges, and promote the well-being of its citizens.

18.1 Healthcare System Overview:

This section provides an overview of Ethiopia's healthcare system, including the structure, organization, and delivery of healthcare services. It examines the roles of the government, healthcare professionals, and the private sector in providing healthcare to the population.

18.2 Healthcare Infrastructure and Facilities:

Access to healthcare facilities is essential for providing quality healthcare services. This chapter discusses the development of healthcare infrastructure, including hospitals, clinics, and health centers, and efforts to expand access to healthcare services in rural and underserved areas.

18.3 Primary Healthcare and Community Health:

Primary healthcare is the foundation of a strong healthcare system. This section explores initiatives to strengthen primary healthcare services, including community-based healthcare delivery, health promotion, disease prevention, and the training of community health workers.

18.4 Disease Prevention and Control:

Preventing and controlling infectious diseases is a critical aspect of public health. This chapter discusses Ethiopia's efforts in disease surveillance, immunization programs, and the control of communicable diseases such as malaria, HIV/AIDS, tuberculosis, and neglected tropical diseases.

18.5 Maternal and Child Health:

Improving maternal and child health is a priority in Ethiopia. This section examines initiatives to reduce maternal and infant mortality, enhance access to prenatal and postnatal care, promote family planning, and address nutritional challenges affecting maternal and child health.

18.6 Non-Communicable Diseases and Chronic Care:

The burden of non-communicable diseases (NCDs) is increasing in Ethiopia. This chapter explores efforts to prevent and manage NCDs such as cardiovascular diseases, diabetes, and cancer. It discusses the integration of NCD care into the healthcare system and the promotion of healthy lifestyle choices.

18.7 Health Information Systems and Technology:

Effective health information systems and technology are crucial for data collection, analysis, and decision-making in healthcare. This section examines the use of technology, electronic health records, and telemedicine in improving healthcare delivery, monitoring public health trends, and enhancing healthcare management.

18.8 Healthcare Workforce Development:

A skilled and motivated healthcare workforce is essential for delivering quality healthcare services. This chapter discusses initiatives to train and retain healthcare professionals, improve their skills through continuous professional development, and address the rural-urban healthcare workforce distribution imbalance.

Conclusion:

Improving healthcare and public health in Ethiopia is vital for the well-being of its population and the country's overall development. By strengthening the healthcare system, expanding access to healthcare services, addressing public health challenges, and investing in healthcare infrastructure and workforce development, Ethiopia can make significant progress in improving health outcomes and achieving universal health coverage. Collaboration with international partners, innovative approaches to healthcare delivery, and a focus on preventative and community-based care will contribute to a healthier and more prosperous Ethiopia.

Chapter 19: Exploring Ethiopian Cuisine: Flavors and Culinary Traditions

In this chapter, we delve deeper into the tantalizing world of Ethiopian cuisine, exploring its diverse flavors, unique ingredients, and culinary traditions. From aromatic spices to communal dining rituals, Ethiopian food offers a sensory experience like no other.

Origins of Ethiopian Cuisine:

Tracing the roots of Ethiopian culinary traditions back to ancient times.
Influence of indigenous ingredients, trade routes, and cultural exchanges on the development of Ethiopian cuisine.

Staple Foods and Iconic Dishes:

Injera: The spongy, sourdough flatbread that serves as the foundation of Ethiopian meals.
Doro Wat: A spicy chicken stew that exemplifies the richness and complexity of Ethiopian flavors.
Tibs: Grilled or sautéed meat dishes seasoned with a variety of spices and herbs.

The Art of Spices and Seasonings:

Berbere: The iconic spice blend that adds depth and heat to many Ethiopian dishes.
Mitmita: A fiery blend of chili peppers, spices, and herbs used to elevate the flavors of grilled meats.
Niter Kibbeh: Ethiopian spiced clarified butter, known for its aromatic qualities and versatility in cooking.

Vegetarian and Vegan Delights:

Shiro: A flavorful stew made from ground legumes, spices, and herbs.
Misir Wat: A rich and hearty lentil stew that is a favorite among vegetarians and vegans.
Atkilt Wat: A vegetable medley stew bursting with flavors and textures.

Coffee Culture and Ceremony:

The Ethiopian coffee ceremony: A revered cultural practice that celebrates the art of coffee preparation and communal bonding.
Ethiopian coffee traditions and the significance of coffee in Ethiopian society.

Regional Culinary Traditions:

Exploring the diverse regional cuisines of Ethiopia, from the spicy dishes of the Amhara and Tigray regions to the milder flavors of the Oromia and Southern Nations.
Unique ingredients and dishes specific to each region.

Modern Innovations and Fusion Cuisine:

The evolution of Ethiopian cuisine in contemporary times, influenced by global culinary trends and creative experimentation.
Ethiopian fusion cuisine and its integration with international flavors.

Ethiopian Beverages:

Tej: Ethiopian honey wine, a traditional fermented beverage enjoyed for its sweet and tangy flavors.
Tella: A traditional Ethiopian beer brewed from barley or wheat.

Ethiopian Culinary Experiences:

Exploring local markets, street food stalls, and restaurants to savor the authentic flavors of Ethiopian cuisine.
Cooking classes and cultural tours that offer visitors a hands-on experience of Ethiopian culinary traditions.
This chapter celebrates the richness of Ethiopian cuisine, its historical significance, and its ability to bring people together in a shared appreciation for flavors and traditions. Whether you are a food enthusiast or simply curious about new culinary experiences, the exploration of Ethiopian cuisine promises a delightful journey of discovery and taste.

Chapter 20: Ethiopian Literature and Poetry: Unveiling Words of Wisdom and Beauty

In this chapter, we embark on a literary journey through the rich tapestry of Ethiopian literature and poetry. From ancient oral traditions to contemporary literary works, Ethiopia has a profound literary heritage that reflects its diverse cultures, languages, and historical experiences.

The Oral Tradition:

The significance of oral storytelling in Ethiopian culture.
Griots and their role as keepers of history, legends, and moral teachings.
Traditional poetic forms, such as the qene and the balageru.

Ancient Texts and Religious Manuscripts:

The importance of religious texts, including the Bible, the Quran, and ancient Ethiopian manuscripts.
The influence of religious texts on Ethiopian literature and poetry.
The tradition of religious chanting and recitation.

Epic Poetry and Folklore:

The epic poem "Kebra Nagast" and its impact on Ethiopian literature.
Folklore and mythical stories that have been passed down through generations.
Folk songs, dances, and rituals associated with storytelling.

Prominent Ethiopian Writers:

Explore the works of renowned Ethiopian authors, such as Tsegaye Gabre-Medhin, Haddis Alemayehu, and Maaza Mengiste.
The themes and motifs prevalent in their literary works.
The influence of Ethiopian history, culture, and socio-political context on their writings.

Modern Ethiopian Literature:

The emergence of modern Ethiopian literature in the 20th century.
The challenges and opportunities faced by Ethiopian writers in the contemporary literary landscape.
Contemporary works that explore themes of identity, migration, social issues, and cultural heritage.

Poetry as an Expression of Ethiopian Identity:

The beauty and power of Ethiopian poetry, from traditional forms to contemporary free verse.
The role of poetry in expressing personal emotions, social commentary, and national identity.
Renowned Ethiopian poets and their contributions to the literary world.

Translations and Global Recognition:

Efforts to translate Ethiopian literature and poetry into other languages.
The impact of translations on promoting Ethiopian literary works to a global audience.
Ethiopian writers and poets who have gained international acclaim.

Literary Festivals and Cultural Events:

The celebration of Ethiopian literature and poetry through literary festivals and cultural events.
The role of these events in nurturing literary talent, fostering dialogue, and preserving Ethiopian literary traditions.

Literary Education and Institutions:

The development of literary education in Ethiopia, including the establishment of writing workshops, creative writing programs, and literary institutions.
The role of literary organizations in promoting Ethiopian literature and supporting aspiring writers.
By exploring the vibrant world of Ethiopian literature and poetry, this chapter sheds light on the voices, wisdom, and creative expressions that have shaped Ethiopian cultural identity. It

showcases the power of words to capture history, evoke emotions, and inspire readers to delve deeper into the rich literary landscape of Ethiopia.

Glossary of Terms

1. Aksum: An ancient kingdom in northern Ethiopia that flourished from the 1st to the 8th century CE and was known for its trade and architectural achievements.
2. Lalibela: A town in northern Ethiopia famous for its rock-hewn churches, which are considered significant religious and architectural landmarks.
3. Griots: Traditional West African storytellers and oral historians who play a vital role in preserving history, culture, and traditions through their narratives.
4. Solomonic Dynasty: The ruling dynasty in Ethiopia, which claims its lineage from the biblical King Solomon and the Queen of Sheba.
5. Qene: A traditional Ethiopian poetic form characterized by its complex and structured patterns of rhyme and meter.
6. Balageru: A form of oral poetry in Ethiopia that involves the exchange of improvised verses between two poets, often accompanied by traditional music and dance.
7. Kebra Nagast: A religious and historical epic poem considered a sacred text in Ethiopian Orthodox Christianity, which narrates the lineage of Ethiopian rulers from King Solomon and the Queen of Sheba.
8. Diaspora: The dispersion of a population from its original homeland, often referring to the Ethiopian diaspora, which consists of Ethiopian individuals and communities living outside of Ethiopia.
9. Timkat: An Ethiopian Orthodox Christian festival celebrated in January, commemorating the baptism of Jesus in the Jordan River.
10. Meskel: A major religious festival in Ethiopia held in September, marking the discovery of the True Cross on which Jesus was crucified, according to Ethiopian Orthodox tradition.
11. Fasil Ghebbi: A royal enclosure in Gondar, Ethiopia, featuring a collection of castles and palaces built during the reign of Emperor Fasilides in the 17th century.
12. Simien Mountains: A mountain range in northern Ethiopia designated as a national park and a UNESCO World Heritage site, known for its stunning landscapes, wildlife, and hiking trails.
13. Ethiopian Orthodox Church: The largest Christian denomination in Ethiopia, known for its distinctive religious practices, rituals, and iconography.
14. Mesob: A traditional Ethiopian dining table, typically made of woven straw or wood, used for serving injera (a sourdough flatbread) and various dishes.
15. Injera: A staple food in Ethiopian cuisine, a sourdough flatbread made from teff flour and served with a variety of stews and dishes.

16. Coffee Ceremony: A traditional Ethiopian ritual of preparing and serving coffee, involving roasting and grinding coffee beans, brewing the coffee, and serving it in small cups.
17. Mesob: A traditional Ethiopian dining table, typically made of woven straw or wood, used for serving injera (a sourdough flatbread) and various dishes.
18. Rock-Hewn Churches: Churches carved out of solid rock, a notable example being the rock-hewn churches of Lalibela in Ethiopia.
19. Ethiopian Orthodox Tewahedo Church: The largest religious denomination in Ethiopia, following the teachings of the Ethiopian Orthodox Church and the Tewahedo doctrine.
20. Axum: An ancient city in northern Ethiopia, once the capital of the Aksumite Kingdom and a major center of trade and civilization.

This glossary provides definitions for key terms related to Ethiopian history, culture, traditions, and religious practices, aiding readers in understanding the specific terminology used throughout the book.

A Song

Translation:

For Ethiopia, a land of great beauty,
To the people who embrace peace with love,
With the warmth of our hearts,
And the wisdom that guides us,
Let us unite in harmony,
Embracing Ethiopia and all its people,
How shall we rise,
How shall we find peace for everyone,
With love in our hearts,
Guided by the Almighty for all to see.

This song, written in Amharic, is a dedication to the people of Ethiopia, expressing the desire for unity, peace, and love among its diverse population Written by **Alok Sharma**

Credit Note

The author would like to express gratitude to the following individuals and organizations whose contributions and support have enriched the creation of this book:

Research Institutions and Libraries: For providing access to valuable resources, historical documents, and literature on Ethiopian history and culture.

Scholars and Experts: For their scholarly insights, knowledge, and guidance in the field of Ethiopian studies, helping to ensure the accuracy and depth of the content.

Ethiopian Communities and Individuals: For sharing their personal stories, experiences, and cultural traditions, providing a firsthand perspective on the rich heritage of Ethiopia.

Editors and Proofreaders: For their meticulous review and editing, ensuring the clarity, coherence, and quality of the book's content.

Friends and Family: For their unwavering support, encouragement, and understanding throughout the writing process.

Readers and Supporters: For their interest, engagement, and appreciation of the subject matter, inspiring the author to delve deeper into the captivating history and culture of Ethiopia.

The author acknowledges the collective effort of all those involved in bringing this book to life and expresses sincere gratitude for their invaluable contributions.

Frequently Asked Questions

Q: Is this book suitable for readers with little knowledge of Ethiopian history and culture?
A: Absolutely! This book is designed to be accessible to readers of all backgrounds, including those with little prior knowledge of Ethiopian history and culture. It provides a comprehensive overview and introduces key concepts, making it an excellent starting point for exploring Ethiopia's rich heritage.

Q: Are there any illustrations or photographs included in the book?
A: Yes, the book includes a collection of carefully selected illustrations and photographs that complement the text and provide visual insights into Ethiopia's history, culture, landmarks, and people.

Q: Does the book cover recent developments and current affairs in Ethiopia?
A: While the book primarily focuses on the historical and cultural aspects of Ethiopia, it also touches upon some significant modern developments. However, please note that the book's content may not be up to date with the most recent events at the time of publication.

Q: Is the book solely focused on Ethiopia's positive aspects, or does it also address challenges and controversies?
A: The book aims to provide a balanced and comprehensive view of Ethiopia, including its achievements, cultural heritage, and diverse traditions. It also acknowledges and addresses some of the challenges and struggles that the country has faced throughout its history. However, readers should note that the book's focus is primarily on highlighting the richness and significance of Ethiopia's history and culture.

Q: Can I use this book as a reference for academic or research purposes?
A: While this book provides a wealth of information, it is not intended as a scholarly or academic reference. It serves as an engaging and accessible introduction to Ethiopian history and culture. For in-depth academic research, it is recommended to consult specialized literature and academic sources.

Q: Is the book available in different formats, such as e-book or audiobook?
A: The availability of different formats may vary depending on the publishing options and platforms. It is advisable to check with the publisher or relevant online platforms for the available formats of the book, such as e-book or audiobook versions.

Q: Can I find additional resources and references for further exploration of Ethiopian history and culture?

A: Absolutely! The book includes a bibliography and recommended reading list that can guide readers to additional resources for further exploration. Additionally, online research, academic journals, and visiting local libraries or cultural centers dedicated to Ethiopian studies can provide valuable resources for in-depth learning.

DISCLAIMER

This book is intended to provide a general overview of the history and culture of Ethiopia. While efforts have been made to ensure the accuracy of the information presented, historical accounts and interpretations can vary, and new discoveries and developments may have emerged since the publication of this book. The author and publisher do not claim to provide an exhaustive or definitive account of Ethiopia's history and culture. Readers are encouraged to consult additional sources and conduct further research for a more comprehensive understanding. The author and publisher shall not be held responsible for any errors, omissions, or any consequences arising from the use of the information contained in this book.